Dropping In On...
ENGLAND

Lewis K. Parker

A Geography Series

ROURKE BOOK COMPANY, INC.
VERO BEACH, FLORIDA 32964

A Blackbirch Graphics book.

Printed in the United States of America.

Library of Congress Cataloging-in-Publication Data

Parker, Lewis K.
    England / Lewis K. Parker.
        p.   cm. — (Dropping in on)
    Includes index.
    ISBN 1-55916-006-3
    1. England—Juvenile literature. [1. England—Description and travel.] I. Title. II. Series: Parker, Lewis K. Dropping in on.
    DA27.5.P37   1994
    941—dc20   94-5471
                                         CIP
                                          AC

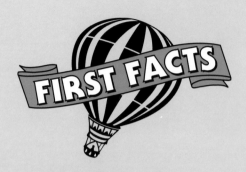

England
· · · · · · · · ·

Official Name: United Kingdom of Great Britain and Northern Ireland

Area: 94,247 square miles

Population: 58,000,000

Capital: London

Largest City: London

Highest Elevation: Ben Nevis (4,406 feet)

Official Language: English

Major Religions: Church of England and Roman Catholic

Money: Pound

Form of Government: Constitutional monarchy

TABLE OF CONTENTS

Our Blue Ball—The Earth

The Earth can be divided into two hemispheres. The word hemisphere means "half a ball"—in this case, the ball is the Earth.

The equator is an imaginary line that runs around the middle of the Earth. It separates the Northern Hemisphere from the Southern Hemisphere. North America—where Canada, the United States, and Mexico are located—is in the Northern Hemisphere.

The Northern Hemisphere

When the North Pole is tilted toward the sun, the sun's most powerful rays strike the northern half of the Earth and less sunshine hits the Southern Hemisphere. That is when people in the Northern Hemisphere enjoy summer. When

the North Pole is tilted away from the sun, and the Southern Hemisphere receives the most sunshine, the seasons reverse. Then winter comes to the Northern Hemisphere. Seasons in the Northern Hemisphere and the Southern Hemisphere are always opposite.

Welcome to England

Hop into your hot-air balloon. Let's take a trip!

You are about to drop in on England, in the Northern Hemisphere. England is one part of the island of Great Britain (Scotland and Wales are the two other parts). England is separated from the continent of Europe by the English Channel and the North Sea and bordered on the southwest by the Atlantic Ocean.

The land in England is mostly gentle and rolling with highlands in the north and west. Flat plains in the east are broken up by small hills. Bleak, empty moors (open, rolling land) are located in the southwest.

Atlantic Ocean

NORTHERN IRELAND

IRELAND

Stop 1: Land's End and Plymouth

Our first stop will be at Land's End and Plymouth. Land's End is the point farthest west in England. It is a very windy place because powerful breezes blow in from the Atlantic Ocean. It is also a place noted for its towering granite cliffs.

In winter, strong ocean winds whip waves up on the cliffs. Off the coast, the Longships Lighthouse blinks warnings to ships passing through.

Not far away is the town of Plymouth. It is an old seaport that was once the home of Sir Francis Drake, a very famous sea captain who was also Plymouth's mayor 400 years ago.

Opposite: Plymouth's Sutton Harbor is always crowded with boats going in and out. Left: The Mayflower Steps in Plymouth were the departure point for the Pilgrims when they left on their voyage to America in 1620.

Because of its natural harbor, Plymouth has a busy waterfront and fishing boats are always tied up to docks. Plymouth has many old houses and narrow streets. Some of these streets lead down to the famous Mayflower Steps.

🎈 *Now we'll travel **northeast** for our second stop in England.*

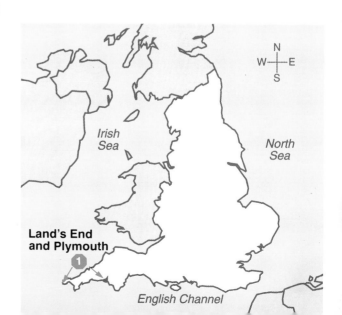

The Roman baths are surrounded by ruins of beautiful Roman buildings.

Irish Sea

North Sea

Bath and Wells

English Channel

Stop 2: Bath and Wells

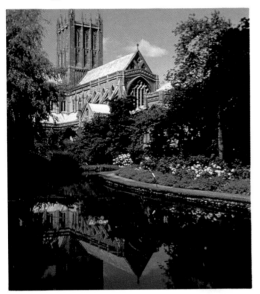

Wells Cathedral.

We have journeyed to England's largest wetland area. This area has many marshes and swamps. Hot water springs gush up from deep underground in the town of Bath. About 1,800 years ago, ancient Romans turned these hot springs into baths.

Not far from the baths is Bath Abbey. The abbey, or church, is a tall building with turrets (small towers) on the front covered with statues of angels.

Wells is another town in this area. Wells is best known for its great cathedral. Inside Wells Cathedral you are surrounded by stained glass and wood carvings. There is a huge clock that is 600 years old. Every hour, several mechanical knights on horseback gallop out of the clock and fight before going back into the clock.

*Now we'll travel **southeast** to Stonehenge.*

Stop 3: Stonehenge

Stonehenge is a group of prehistoric ruins. There are 162 gray-green stone blocks. Some are standing and some are lying down. A barbed wire fence keeps visitors away from the blocks so they can be seen, but not touched.

No one knows why the stones were placed here. They could be arranged to form a kind of calendar. The stones are placed in line with a point at which the sun rises above the horizon on the first day of summer. The stones could also have been a kind of cemetery. The bodies of people have been found under some of the stones.

The stone blocks of Stonehenge were arranged 4,000 years ago.

🎈 *For our next stop, we'll travel* **northeast** *to London.*

Irish
Sea

North
Sea

Stonehenge

English Channel

Stop 4: London

London is the capital city of England and one of the greatest cities in the world. The Thames River divides London into a northern part and a southern part.

We might want to begin our visit to London in the Westminster section.

Trafalgar Square is named after the Battle of Trafalgar in 1805. During this battle, Lord Nelson defeated the French fleet off the coast of Spain.

Nearby is Buckingham Palace, where the royal family lives. The Changing of the Guard in front of the palace is fun to watch. The guards wear uniforms with tall hats and they never change the expressions on their faces.

While we are in this part of the city, you won't be able to help hearing Big Ben, a huge clock that is on top of the Palace of Westminster. The bell of this clock weighs more than 13 tons. Beneath Big Ben is England's Parliament—where laws are made. The British Parliament is the oldest parliament in the world.

Opposite: Big Ben was named after Sir Benjamin Hall, Commissioner of Works in 1859.

Westminster Abbey is also located in this part of London. This is the church where royal weddings are held. Kings and queens are buried here along with the country's important statesmen, soldiers, scientists, musicians, and authors.

Within London's business district is St. Paul's Cathedral. The dome of the cathedral looks like a giant cup from the outside. Inside, you can take the stairs up to the Whispering Gallery. If you put an ear against the wall, you can hear a whisper from over 100 feet away.

Farther away is the Tower of London, which is on the banks of the Thames River. The tower is closely guarded by Yeomen Warders—also known as Beefeaters—who dress in costumes.

The west end of London is well known for its theaters, restaurants, department stores, and shops. You might want to visit Piccadilly Circus where the city's neon lights shine day and night.

Just west of Piccadilly is Mayfair. Park Lane, a busy street in Mayfair, is lined with hotels. A path from the street leads to the Serpentine, an artificial lake, in Hyde Park. There you can sunbathe or sit on the beach. You can also visit the London Zoo in Regent's Park.

Coronation ceremonies are held at Westminster Abbey.

Next, *we'll head* **northwest** *to the Peak District.*

Stop 5: Peak District

You'll probably notice that the environment changes as we enter the Peak District. We are in England's first national park. It is a wild area that covers about 450 square miles. The northern areas

The beautiful countryside of the Peak District makes it a great place for hiking and bike riding.

have gloomy moors and oddly shaped mountains bordered by long walls of gray rock. There are not many villages and few people live here. The central and southern areas have rolling hills and lush valleys. Bright flowers dot the green pastures and the air is clean.

One place to visit is Chatsworth, which is the grand home to the dukes of Devonshire. This magnificent mansion is often open to the public for tours.

Haddon Hall.

Haddon Hall is another huge and stately mansion. It is built on a bluff above the Wye River. The banquet hall and kitchen look the same as they did 500 years ago!

LET'S TAKE TIME OUT

These English schoolchildren are on a museum field trip to London.

Growing Up in England

If you lived in England, you would start school at age 5. In the lower grades, you would study reading, writing, arithmetic, and other subjects. At age 11, you would begin secondary school and study a foreign language and science.

At home, your evening meal might be a meat dish, vegetables, and a dessert. Meat dishes are often chicken, pork, or lamb. Shepherd's pie (lamb with herbs and onions and mashed potatoes on top) is one type of meat dish. "Bubble and squeak" (corned beef with cabbage and mashed potatoes that are fried until crisp) is also popular. Another dish, "bangers and mash" (sausages with mashed potatoes), is a typical English meal.

After school, you might play cricket or rugby, which is similar to football. The main sport is soccer, which is called football in England.

*Now we'll set sail and travel slightly **southwest** to Liverpool.*

Stop 6: Liverpool

Liverpool is a seaport noted for its waterfront. Its docks are mainly empty now, but some of the warehouses have been turned into apartments and shops. There are a group of palaces near the Lime Street railway station. The largest of the palaces is St. George's Hall. It holds the law court and the concert hall. Another important building here is the Anglican Cathedral. It took 75 years to build and wasn't completed until 1978. It's one of the last and biggest of the Gothic-style cathedrals.

While we're in Liverpool, you might want to take the Beatles' Magical History Tour. It's a tour of the key places in the lives of this rock group, which came from Liverpool.

Now we'll travel **northeast** to York.

The Maritime Museum in Liverpool is an interesting place to visit.

The Rievaulx Abbey is in the north of York.

Stop 7: York

York is an ancient city with swampy soil. The history of this area has been preserved well. The city was built as the headquarters of the Roman army. The original streets were buried under the highways that run through York.

The narrow streets of the city lead like a maze around York Minster. This is the largest Gothic cathedral in northern Europe. It took about 250 years to build.

Just north of York, the flat land turns into a plateau. Villages are scattered among the hills and valleys. This is where you'll discover Rievaulx Abbey. The monks who once lived here were the first large-scale sheep farmers in England.

North York Moors is a national park here that covers 500 square miles. It is the only national park to touch the North Sea. It receives the least rainfall of any park in England. Here you'll see rolling heather moors, small valleys, and a spectacular seacoast.

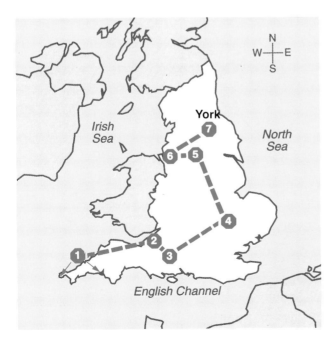

*For our final stop, we will travel **northwest** to visit the scenic Lake District.*

Stop 8: Lake District

The Lake District may be the most scenic part of England. It is not a large area, but it has moors, mountain roads, valleys, waterfalls, and lakes.

The lakes in this area were formed at the end of the Ice Age, about 10,000 years ago. Huge glaciers blocked running rivers. These rivers formed pools and then lakes. The largest lake in England, Lake Windermere, is found here.

A few miles from the western side of Lake Windermere is the cottage where Beatrix Potter

You can take a boat trip on Lake Windermere from the Ambleside pier.

lived in the early 1900s. She was the author of the Peter Rabbit books.

The poet William Wordsworth also lived in the Lake District. The village of Grasmere still looks as it did when Wordsworth was a boy.

Now it's time to set sail for home. When you return, you can think back on the wonderful adventure you had in England.

English Words

Although people in England speak English just as you do, there are several differences in the meanings of the words they use. Here are some differences:

American	English
hood (of car)	bonnet
trunk (of car)	boot
pharmacy, druggist	chemist
apartment	flat
elevator	lift
truck	lorry
sidewalk	pavement
baby carriage	pram
stroller	pushchair
gasoline	petrol
private school	public school
doctor or dentist's office	surgery
candy	sweet
flashlight	torch
subway	underground

Further Reading

Binney, Don. *Inside Great Britain*. New York: Franklin Watts, Inc., 1988.

Licata, Renora. *Princess Diana: Royal Ambassador*. Woodbridge, CT: Blackbirch Press, 1992.

Macaulay, David. *Cathedral*. Boston: Houghton Mifflin, 1981.

Marker, Sherry. *London*. Woodbridge, CT: Blackbirch Press, 1992.

Maynard, Christopher. *Castles*. New York: Kingfisher Books, 1993.

Stadtler, Christa. *The United Kingdom*. New York: Franklin Watts, Inc., 1992.

Thibault, Dominique. *Long Ago in a Castle*. Lake Forest, IL: Forest House Publishing Company, 1993.

Index

Acknowledgments and Photo Credits
Cover: ©Louis Goldman/Photo Researchers, Inc.; pp. 4, 6: National Aeronautics and Space Administration; pp. 10, 11, 16, 19, 20, 25, 26, 28: ©Mirror Syndication International; pp. 12, 13, 15, 21: Courtesy of the British Tourist Authority; p. 22: ©Jeff Greenberg/Photo Researchers, Inc. Maps by Blackbirch Graphics, Inc.

	DATE DUE		
3/27/00			